Fun

Ruchi mehta

BookLeaf
Publishing

India | USA | UK

Dedication

Preface

Acknowledgements

1. Autumn Leaves

Autumn coloured leaves
Dancing on the tree branches
Serenity and wonder
The end is near now
Brown is the colour of death
Time spares nothing at the end

2. Sunny Day

A beautiful sunny afternoon
Sunlight filtering through the trees
Silence prevails all around
Birds chirping in the trees
Gentle breeze blowing
Rustling of leaves
Feel hopeful
About
Life

3. The Wizard

A wizard with long white beard
Casting spells with a pen
Was known by all and feared
As he could turn men into hen
The wizard had a pet gnat
Which he took for a walk in the park
A clown slipped and squished it flat
The wizard's mood grew dark
"Abracadabra, hocus pocus
Magic words, flying high
Buzzing here, now focus
Turn the clown into a fly"
Spoof! The clown turned into a fly
Everyone was filled with dread
The wizard walked off with a sigh
With a fly buzzing around his head

4. Upside Down

I woke up to see
My slippers on the ceiling
I looked out of the window
It sent me reeling
People walking on the roof
Upturned trees
Fish in the sky
Cars driving in the seas
 I went looking for my mum
But she was not to be seen
I yelled out her name
And joined the upside-down scene

5. Summer Journey

Path

People

All hustling

Cooking dinner

Familiar smells waft

A gentle evening breeze

Birds chirping as they return

Twinkling stars lighting up the sky

Rice plants dancing, whispering softly

A feeling of dread as we draw nearer

6. Clumsy Fish

Clumsy Fish wore a bow tie

For a party in Mumbai

He fell into a puddle

Got out with a struggle

But his bow tie stayed dry

7. Owl and Tree

In the dense forests of Flee

There lived a very old oak tree

All day long it would mutter

About how it hated the stinky gutter

A little owl came to stay

And asked the tree if it wanted to play

"I'm way too old for that

Would you rather have a chat

Tell me about the stars you see at night

I'll whisper the secrets of the forest's might"

8. Fly

There was a tiny mouse from Grouse

In the clouds he built a new house

He wanted wings to fly

So he could live in the sky

But he was awakened by his spouse

9. Sand like Status

slimy slug
slimy sand
sand storm
sand shoes
shoes size
shoes storage
storage solutions
storage space
space ships
space stations
station square
station street
street skater
street signs
signs showing shock
signs showing stroke
stroke specialist
stroke support
support system
support staff
staff survey
staff schedule
schedule software
schedule sleep

sleep stages

sleep solutions

solutions specialist

solutions science

science syllabus

science symbols

symbols smiley

symbols star

star signs

star shape

shape shooter

shape sorter

sorter system

sorter software

software support

software store

store security

store supply

supply solutions

supply shipment

shipment services

shipment status

status saver

status symbol

symbol

saver

10. Black Cat

In Shadow Town lives a fat, black cat

He is very fond of his tall hat

He can't wear it now

He's lost it somehow

He is searching all his habitat

11. Beach Crab

When I went to the beach
In the month of June
I met a fat crab
Balancing a big peach
On a small spoon
While skating on a marble slab

12. Duck and Gnat

Missy Duck wore a long top hat
On top of the hat sat a gnat
The gnat was grumpy
The duck was dumpy
When suddenly it fell with a splat!

13. Night Sky

The cloudless night sky
Dotted with bright twinkling stars
Always enchants me
Fill the darkest night with light
The shadows will fall behind

14. Jealousy

Jealousy is born of insecurity
Evades unmasking by victims
Afflicted men bid sanity adieu
Lusts for others' possessions with gusto
Often without heed comes to dwell
Usually its intent is an enigma
Such an ugly nature
Yes, it is not at all GORJ

15. The Trip

I went on a trip
With friends and my family

We started at dawn
So we hardly slept at night

The sky was golden
Empty road stretched before us

Songs of my past played
On the drive to the

Tall trees lined the road
Wearing autumn colours proudly

The sky changing colours
Was better than any painting

16. Puns

Puns

Are fun

They can daze

And then amaze

I find them witty

Specially when bitty

They say more in fewer words

So they are mostly my passwords

Here is an example that I like

Don't trust atoms. They make up everything

17. Morning Walk

Morning walk

Me time

Golden glow from the rising sun

Solitude in the midst of nature

Birds chirping

Leaves crunching

Soul refreshed

18. Ghost

There was a grumpy ghost
Who lived on the seacoast
He would always boast
That he was the best host
And flattery he loved the most
He was addicted to toast
That he ate with pork roast
This is the winning post
Delivered by parcel post
Straight from the Gold Coast

19. Norwesters in Summer

Nothing matches its savage strength
Occurring in late summer afternoons
Rolling in with a roar
'

Worth watching from the window
Easily uprooting trees
Scaring birds into hiding
Thunder and lightning are its cohorts
Entrancing man with its might
Rain is a faithful follower
Sweeps away all melancholy

20. Seeds

Seeds,
are mothers,
birthing the new plants,
nurturing and protecting.
Maturing to reproduce,
new life cycle starts,
plants start to,
seed.

21. Volcano

Fire spewing mountain
Hot molten sun flowing down
Nurturing black ash

Loud fiery monster
Chasing and destroying all
Entices tourists